ELYNN O'HEATHER

HR INTERVIEW SECRETS

**The Ultimate Insider Guide to the Best Interview Practices,
Learn the Tips and Tricks On How to
Ace Modern Interviews Successfully**

AF287973

Descrierea CIP a Bibliotecii Naționale a României
ELYNN O'HEATHER
    HR INTERVIEW SECRETS. The Ultimate Insider Guide
to the Best Interview Practices, Learn the Tips and Tricks On
How to Ace Modern Interviews Successfully / Elynn O'Heather –
Bucharest: Editura My Ebook, 2020
    ISBN 978-606-983-607-1

ELYNN O'HEATHER

HR INTERVIEW SECRETS

The Ultimate Insider Guide to the Best Interview Practices, Learn the Tips and Tricks On How to Ace Modern Interviews Successfully

My Ebook Publishing House
Bucharest, 2020

TABLE OF CONTENT

CHAPTER 1

IMPORTANCE OF KNOWING THE TIPS
AND TRICKS FOR INTERVIEWS

So, you've recently passed your graduation and are looking for a job. Thousands of others are doing the same and may be that the job you are applying for already has over 20 applicants. All of them have the same qualification and experience. They also read the same sample questions and prepare in a similar manner for the job interview. So, how can you differentiate yourself from the rest? How can you ensure that you get noticed by the interviewers and they pick you from the crowd?

This e-book mainly aims at giving you an edge over the usual practice for the interviews. Knowing the tips and tricks of the interviews makes you more confident and helps you to handle all sorts of questions. You can do a brainstorming and list down all sort of questions- common, uncommon, and weird that could possibly be asked.

Sometimes candidates are put in a situation when they may not like to answer a particular question. Sometimes the questions are tricky and you need to be really careful while answering them. In such circumstances, it becomes very important to know how to deal with the situation and what to say. The tips and tricks help you learn these tactics so that you can face all sorts of situations when in an interview.

While in an interview it is very important to keep some important things in mind such as:

✓ What to wear and how this can be determined

✓ Proper preparation for the interview

✓ How to handle the tricky questions

✓ How to draft a winning resume

✓ What to say and what to abstain from during the interview

✓ Learn the tricks to judge the interviewer by their tone of voice and body language.

All the above mentioned points are extremely important to help a candidate face all kinds of odds that he or she may face in an interview. If you look for answers you may find several answers online for the above mentioned questions. However, our aim is to create one platform from where you can get a set of reliable answers and tips for a better career.

CHAPTER 2

THE DIFFERENT TYPES OF INTERVIEWS

The basic framework of an interview is of course the same and it take place when there is an interviewer and interviewee. However, the pattern of the interviews may vary depending upon the requirement and the situation under which the interview is held. Basically, there are four different types of interviews differentiated on the basis of a wide variety of factors. The interview patterns include:

- ✓ Phone Interview
- ✓ Panel Interview
- ✓ Exit Interview
- ✓ Lunch Interview

2.1. **Phone Interview:**

It may seem that partaking in a phone interview can help in taking off the pressure that is build up in the process; however this is not always true. The phone interviews are looked upon as the informal means by which a candidate can get a job. However, unfortunately, the candidates make some of the most critical mistakes when dealing with the questions asked in a phone interview. First of all it is important to deeply understand the increasing popularity of this type of interview. Some of the main factors that make phone interviews really special include:

✓ Time is in fact one of the biggest factors as it saves the time of the interviewer as well as the one who is being interviewed.

✓ It also helps judging a potential candidate before actually calling him or her for the interview. It helps as a time saving technique.

✓ It helps in clarifying any confusion regarding the post before a formal interview.

✓ It helps the interviewee to discuss the position and inquire about the additional career information.

However the drawback of this kind of interview is that although it caters to the immediate needs of the employers, it sometimes is not as good for the interviewee. At times, such interviews can be really bad for the candidates as they can leave him/ her panting for breath and trying to catch the phone off guard, for even the quite simple questions. Bad network and unfavorable surroundings of the candidate can also cause hurdles in the meeting.

2.2. Panel Interview:

Just like the phone interviews, the panel interviews are getting high on popularity. The need for this type of interview mainly rises from the need to stretch the time over multiple numbers of tasks. The process and procedures of holding a meeting are also getting modified so that all those people who all involved in the recruitment process can a meet, judge, discuss, and take a discuss.

The panel interview can be one of the most stressful of all other types of interviews. The candidate is mostly put into several questions from different people and the candidate has a tough job in pleasing all the judges in the interview panel. Relating to the interviewers can become just impossible in this case.

Here are some tips that can really help you to face a panel interview:

✓ Come with a cheat sheet as a part of your preparation. This should contain the highlights of all the things that you wish to mention in your interview. It should mainly focus on all sorts of key assets. Remember that when asked to mention your key elements; don't write an essay on it. Just give an outline on what needs to be mentioned there.

✓ It is a known truth that people like hearing their name during a conversation. When you come for an interview and you know that it is a panel type, remember to pay attention to their names. Take note of the names and use them during your conversation and while asking or answering questions.

✓ Another wonderful tip for the panel interviews or any group conversation is to cross reference the last question asked with the questions that have been asked before. This will help making you comfortable and answering to more than one person at the same time.

✓ It could be that during the interview, the panel of judges may mention things that may be worth remembering so carry a note pad with you. If you take notes of the important things mentioned by the interviewers then it makes them feel important and t also gives a good impression of you as being responsible and careful. This will also help to ensure that you don't forget any part of the important facts mentioned in the interview.

✓ Making proper eye contact is considered as very important in an interview, and when it is a panel interview the candidate has to be much more careful as he/ she has to face many people at the same time. When someone asks you a question, don't just stare at him/ her while answering. You must make more eye contact with the person who asked you the question, but at the same time, also look at other people in the panel.

One of the major drawbacks of the panel interviews is that it can be quite stressful for the job seekers as they may feel a bit out numbered. You must always keep in mind that you are an asset to their business and they feel that you are really important, otherwise they wouldn't have all gathered here to interview. Therefore, the key to success here is to stay as calm as you can and take your time and answer all the questions effectively.

2.3. **Lunch Interview**

This is a rather "laid back" form of interview and generally named to those types of interviews which are held somewhere close to the meal/ lunch time. This kind of interviews is generally taken between friends, ex-colleagues, or sometimes when it is just final test before passing the signal for the winning candidate.

The main advantage of this kind of interview is that it has a lax setting, which can provide an open forum for frankness. Here, the candidate can be at ease and answer according to his heart's content and he doesn't necessarily have to sound just like what the employer wants him to be.

However, there is a disadvantage when it comes to confidence. Some people are really nervous when there are people watching him/ her eat. A confident eater knows that he can handle all sorts of situations and if there is a mess, he can just smartly grab a napkin and clear it off. However, a nervous character person would find it really tough to concentrate on anything g else other than the spot.

While on a lunch interview you need to take extra care on how you handle food and everything as this may reflect your personality and style too. You need some practice for this beforehand. However, here are some tips that will help you get success in a lunch interview:

✓ Order something simple to eat, like bread. You can break down the bread into smaller pieces and convenient bites

✓ Try to avoid having anything other than water that can spill. Remember to never order or suggest any kind of alcoholic beverages, even if the person interviewing you does)

✓ Try to order something similar also to your interviewer

✓ Always wipe your mouth using a napkin and try to avoid eating anything for which you may have to use picking teeth.

✓ You must always be careful to not use your fingers while eating unless your lunch meal consists of sandwich or some finger food

Mostly the company pays for the lunch meals, but if you are going for such interviews then ensures that you have enough money to pay for both yours and your interviewer's meal along with the tip if you have to.

You must thank your interviewer with a firm handshake after the lunch. Most of the times people do not send a thank you note after the lunch interviews. Make yourself different from the rest; send out a 'Thank you' note.

2.4. **Exit interview:**

The exit type of interview is generally held when an individual leaves a particular company and hence it is named as an 'exit interview'. However, not all companies follow the process of interviewing all their former employees. But those companies who wish to build relationships and re-structure and reform their in house policies, usually go for such kind of practices.

The time frames of the exit interviews are generally the same and they are usually performed during the last days of the candidate's employment. Sometimes, the exit interviews are even performed some 2 to 3 months after the individual leaves the employment.

Advantages of having exit interviews:

✓ It helps in focusing light on the outgrown policies and procedures

✓ It helps in determining the employee's state of mind

✓ It cats as a sound forum to discuss future re-employment or arbitrate difficulties

✓ It helps in identifying the departmental competencies or unsuitability

✓ It picks the conflicts / complications that may be harmful for employees and management

Disadvantages of the exit interview:

✓ It may bring forth any kind of inter personal conflicts as well as the gossip sessions

✓ It becomes tough to maintain an optimistic or positive mood, if the candidate was fired

✓ It provides a ground for aggressive or irrational employees to vent out their anger which may be disruptive.

CHAPTER 3

SKILL BUILDING TO CRACK INTERVIEWS

'Skill building' is an important terminology that greatly helps when it comes to cracking interviews. Skill building is an art that cannot be taught in any school or college. They only impart knowledge to you. It depends on you how well you build your skills depending on the knowledge that you have gained throughout the years.

Skill building is no rocket science or anything hi- fi. Some practice and patience can help you build your skills. Some of the important aspects that can help you building your skills are:

Give time to practice your 'writing skills' – Today's internet world is fast and demanding. You need to have really good writing skills to excel. Documentation is an important aspect and your writing skills reflect in your emails to potential employers. It also shows in your cover letters and 'thank you' letters. This shows that having good communication skill is very crucial and vital.

Keeping yourself informed and up breast with all the day to day happenings is another important aspect that you must take into consideration. Keep yourself updated by reading magazines, newspapers and blogs. Make it a habit to spend some time everyday to know what is happening in the world outside. You can also use the feed subscription tools such as Newsgator Online Edition and Bloglines.

Writing resume effectively is an art that you need to build. If by any case you cannot crack the first interview that you face, consider taking a refresher course before you think about re-writing your resume.

You may also stat a blog and use it as a medium to demonstrate and share your knowledge in a topic with others. This will help other job seekers and may even get you noticed by potential employers.

Social networking is a great platform to learn from other's mistakes and build your skills. Interact with people in the forums, make friends and build your skill set.

CHAPTER 4

TOOLS AND MISCELLANEOUS YOU NEED TO HAVE

If you are looking for a job, or are planning to go for an interview then there are some tools that you need to have so that you are ready for it. They need not be too costly but should be professional enough to make you look smart and ready for the job. The tools manly consist f the following:

The Must Haves:

A Laptop or a Computer: You may either buy one or borrow to get your work done. But, you require a compute or a laptop to type your resume, the cover letter and the reference pages. This is essential to get ready for the job.

Easy access to the Internet: Your job search mainly depends on how much time you spend searching for the jobs online. You must post your updated resume in the major job portals in the World Wide Web. If you already have it posted then you must remember to keep updating it to be always intimated about the new job openings.

A portfolio or briefcase: This is necessary for protecting your things and materials against any damage when you attend a job fair or go out for an interview.

A mobile phone: If you are in desperate need of a job then you must always be contactable no matter where you are. So, if you have posted your resume in the job portals then chances are that they may want to contact you. Under these circumstances, you must always be reachable and the best way to ensure this is to always carry a mobile phone with you.

CHAPTER 5

THE RIGHT 'RESUME' – SIGNIFICANCE AND IMPORTANCE

A good resume is the key to your getting successful with interviews at one shot. Most of the interviewers create a perception about the candidate by just looking at the resume. A good and effective looking resume gives a positive impression about you, whereas a poorly written resume can get you rejected even before you attend the interview. An average result shows that an employer usually spends not more than 30 seconds to see a resume and this is the time for you to prove yourself worthy for the job and create the much needed first good impression. This explains why the resume is so significant and carries so much of importance. Some of the important things that you musty keep in mind while drafting a resume are:

Never lie when you are writing your resume, as this may cost you later. Mention all your skills, qualifications, and experiences, carefully and honestly.

Try to make resume sound relevant. Don't lists down the names and birthdays of your parents out there. It is not your personal diary. Instead, make it more related to your profile and job.

Keep two to three resume that are customized for your different job requirements. Depending upon the type of industry, you can use different types of resume.

There are several types of formats available for drafting resume. You can follow a standard format to draft your resume. The fresh grads should always emphasize on their degrees and grades. Where as the experienced candidates should give the details of the previous job experience

The resume should be easy to read so try to avoid using complicated sentences and jargons. Make use of bullets and tables to make it easy to understand and read. Always use the right words; you can use industry terms, but avoid being too academic with the lingo.

Try to promote yourself with your resume and it should have the capability to sell you to the employers. Don't make it sound to bragging but use the correct words to emphasize your skills.

Always gives some good references in the resume who can be contacted easily and quickly. Someone in a good position and who knows you well should be given in references. Remember to never give out false references as this may back fire and cause much harm to your career.

Highlight all your interests in your resume because this helps the interviewers to judge your personality and character.

After you are done drafting the resume, proofread, check for spellings and grammar and get it printed in good quality paper.

CHAPTER 6

PREPARING PROPERLY FOR AN INTERVIEW

Preparation plays an important role when it comes to seeking a job or going for an interview. The preparation of an interview is quite crucial and this may determine your confidence and success level. If you are well prepared the chances are you will be more confident to face the interview. On the other hand if you go without nay preparation then you may feel nervous to even attend the interview. Here are some ways that can help you prepare well for an interview:

Ask your family and friends: This is the best way to lean and prepare for an interview. You need to learn from other people's mistakes. Ask them to give you some valuable advice, tips and suggestions. This will help you get geared up for the interview.

You can also ask for suggestions and advice in any social gatherings if you are unable to find the right person to help you.

Ask people in the church, they would surely give you a lead to help you out and assist you in preparing for an interview.

If you are still in college then take suggestions from your professors and seniors. They may give you the right advice and help you prepare.

If you are looking for a job then you can ask your seniors and former classmates. They may have vacancies in the company that they work with. There are many companies who pay for referrals so your friends could also be benefited by referring you.

Try out the social networking sites for more helps as there are forums where peers offer advice. Check out the groups that discuss job, interviews etc.

You can also join the career websites like LinkedIn or JibberJobber, and ask for help.

The job fairs are a good learning experience. Try to attend as many job fairs as you can and try meeting more companies and people there. This also helps a great deal in preparing you for the job market. Always carry your résumé and cover letters when you go to a job fair.

Always keep checking the newspapers and job portal sites for latest information and news.

CHAPTER 7

WHAT ROLE DOES APPEARANCE PLAY?

You may wonder is appearance at all plays any importance while seeking a job. Just imagine that you are an interviewer and you find a candidate walking up to you in jeans and T-shirt, unshaven hair and smelling bad. Would you like to think even twice before rejecting that guy? Well, the same is the case with you if you are not properly dressed or shaved.

No matter how good your qualifications are, they are checked later. The first thing that the interviewer notices when you walk into the room is you, and your outward experience and you need to create an impact with this. Here are some important tips to ensure that you appear right for an interview:

Always practice your entry walk and handshake in front of the mirror, the night before you go for the interview. Check out your facial expressions and see if it is good enough to impress.

Keep your dress ready and well ironed for the day. Don't wear new clothes as they may be uncomfortable. Always wear comfortable and professional looking dresses. Men should always ensure that they wear a tie. Shoes should be buffed and neat.

Women should avoid wearing too much of jewellery or too gaudy a dress.

Don't go for an entire makeover before the interview. A new haircut may make you conscious or uneasy. Just be comfortable and be as you are. Men should avoid spikes or colored hairs. Get enough sleep so that your eyes are not red.

Brush your teeth well so that you don't have bad breath. Use a light perfume to smell good.

CHAPTER 8

TIPS TO GEAR UP - PRE-INTERVIEW

On the day before the interview you must be feeling very nervous and may have butterflies in your stomach. Here are some tips that can help you prepare better for "The Day":

Know the address well, check for nay details and landmarks if required. Ensure that you will be able to reach in time. If you are in doubt, check the company website and call them for details.

Know the answers to the sure t be asked questions such as why have you come for the interview. Know the answers whether it is small, big, cool job etc.

Remember to arrive early at the interview place. Coming 10 minutes early is enough, no need to come too early. Greet the receptionist and inform your arrival.

Don't smoke while you wait for your turn. Take the restroom beforehand and put your cell on silence if required.

8.1. Things To Remember For The Interview

Remember that your behaviors and impression is an important judgmental factor during your interview. Your qualification and experience is already there on the resume. So, what are the interviewers looking for? They want to check your style, behavior and personality. Here are some tips for a good interview behavior:

✓ Knock before you enter the room

✓ Wait for the handshake with the employer. The handshake should be a firm one, not bones breaking but with a good grip.

✓ Don't sit until the person in front of you asks you to take a seat.

✓ Always keep a pleasant appearance and wear a genuine smile on your face.

✓ Always create the first good impression and maintain it till your leave the room.

8.2. The Do's and Don'ts of Interview

While going for an interview it is very important to keep in mind the dos and don'ts of the interview. Here are the main ones:

Dos:

✓ Always maintain good eye contact while talking with the interviewer.

✓ Be concise and clear with your answers, avoid any beating around the bush.

✓ You may nod your head to answer at times but don't over do this.

✓ If you don't understand a question then always ask for clarifications.

✓ When given a chance to ask questions, ask about the things that the interviewer has not mentioned.

✓ Be flexible with your skills and don't wring your nose at anything.

✓ Ask about your role and the team that you will be working with.

✓ You may also ask about your future growth and opportunities in the organization.

Don'ts:

✓ Don't let your first question be about the salary and benefits.

✓ Don't fiddle with anything as this is considered unhealthy

✓ Don't mumble while you are speaking, be audible and clear.

✓ Don't seem as if you are intimidated or scared.

✓ Don't appear as if you are arrogant.

✓ Don't lie under any circumstances whatsoever.

✓ Don't show off try to overreact on anything.

✓ Don't hit try to hit on your interviewer under any circumstance. Remember that you're in interview, not a club.

✓ Don't complain about your previous boss or company.

✓ Don't seem too needy for the job as it may not help you.

CHAPTER 9

MODERN TIPS BY INTERVIEW EXPERTS

One that you are almost geared for the interview; here are some modern tips from the experts that can help you in the long run:

✓ Take care to not pass on too much of your personal information to the secretary, the interviewer, or any member of the company where you have come for interview.

✓ Focus on yourself and the interview; keep away from personal habits if you have any, like habit of tapping of feet, biting nails, and twitching.

✓ If you know the interviewer name then use it during your conversation. This makes a good impression and helps you create a good impression.

✓ Always sit or stand in a good posture. Your body language can speak a lot about your personality and character.

✓ Talk to the interviewer confidently and ask him any company or job related questions if you wish.

✓ Don'tappear artificial; just relax and keep your calm when you are being interviewed.

9.1. How To Close An Interview From Your Side

After you are almost done the closing of the interview also creates an impact so be careful with it. When asked about when you can join be confident and give your date. Don't hesitate to mention any leave or vacation that you already have scheduled. Discuss any salary issue if you need to. Get all your queries cleared before leaving the room.

Before leaving, thank the interviewer for his/ her time and shake hands properly. Smile and exit the room gracefully. Smile at the secretary or receptionist and thank her too. Remember to send a thank you letter after you go back.

9.2. Conclusion

Although the job market is tough and competitive, there are no stops for the right candidate. If you have it in you, all you need is to add a little edge to it to stand out from the others. Your resume and your words should be effective enough to sell you in the right manner and in the right place. I hope this e-book with all the compiled instructions and details about how to face a modern interview and crack it will help you achieve confidence and success.

9 786069 836330

Printed by
Libri Plureos GmbH · Friedensallee 273
22763 Hamburg · Germany